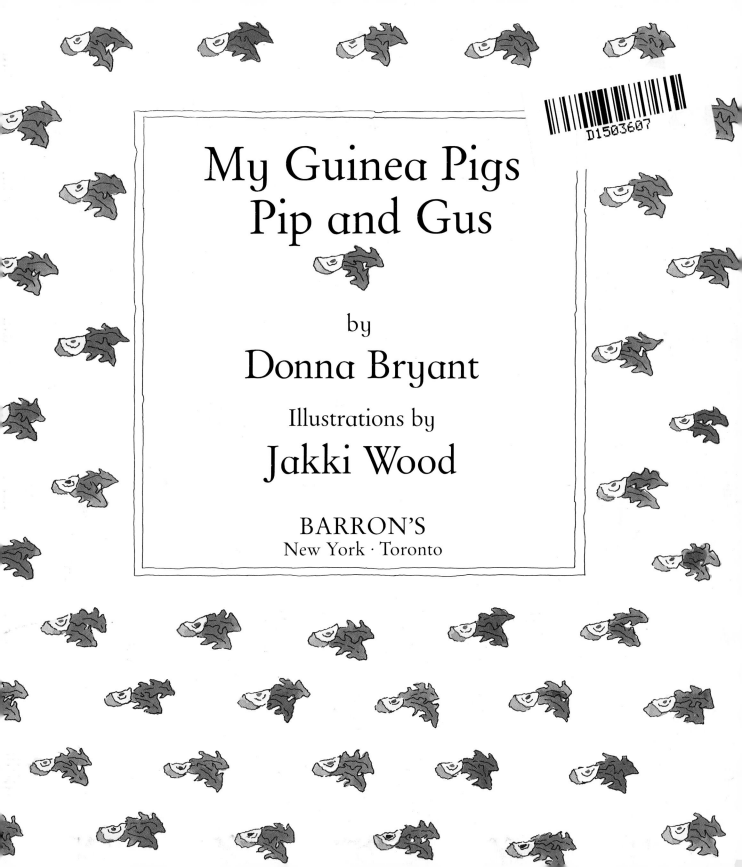

My Guinea Pigs
Pip and Gus

by

Donna Bryant

Illustrations by

Jakki Wood

BARRON'S
New York · Toronto

My guinea pigs are called Pip and Gus.

They are a lot of fun!

Pip and Gus squeak when they see me.

I tickle them under the chin and
they chuckle.

They spend a lot of time eating...

and they love to sleep.

But they wake up when they see
dandelion leaves,

and they love to chew on a carrot
or an apple.

They like it when I let them out of their cage.

They can run even faster than me!

When I lie down on the grass

I can see their big teeth and pink lips.

Pip and Gus don't like loud noises,

but they like it when I sing softly.

Guinea pigs have beautiful babies.

They look just like their parents.

Guinea pigs are the most gentle pets
in the world.

I love my guinea pigs.

First edition for the United States, Canada, and the Philippines
published 1991 by Barron's Educational Series, Inc.

Text © Copyright 1991 by Donna Bryant
Illustrations © Copyright 1991 by Jakki Wood

My Guinea Pigs Pip and Gus was conceived, edited, and produced by
Frances Lincoln Ltd, Apollo Works, 5 Charlton Kings Road,
London NW5 2SB

All inquiries should be addressed to:
Barron's Educational Series, Inc.
250 Wireless Boulevard
Hauppauge, New York 11788

International Standard Book No. 0-8120-6213-2
Library of Congress Catalog Card No. 90-47923

Library of Congress Cataloging-in-Publication Data
Bryant, Donna.
  My guinea pigs Pip and Gus / by Donna Bryant : Illustrations by
Jakki Wood. 1st ed.
    p. cm.
  Summary: A boy describes how he feeds, cares for, and loves his
pet guinea pigs Pip and Gus.
  ISBN 0-8120-6213-2
  [1. Guinea pigs–Fiction.] I. Wood, Jakki, ill. II. Title.
PZ7.B837My   1991
(E)–dc20   90-47923
                                                            CIP
                                                            AC
PRINTED IN HONG KONG
1234 0987654321